From
Home
to
Sunset

From
Home
to
Sunset

Poems by

Derek William Stead

Library of Congress Control Number: 2018900135
ISBN: Hardcover   978-1-5434-8707-7
                   Softcover   978-1-5434-8706-0
                   eBook   978-1-5434-8705-3

Print information available on the last page.

Rev. date: 01/11/2018

To order additional copies of this book, contact:
Xlibris
800-056-3182
www.Xlibrispublishing.co.uk
Orders@Xlibrispublishing.co.uk
764922

Contents

Introduction...xi

The Fortunes of War 1
Home..2
The Raven..3
Pie 4
A Hero of Conscience...5
The Wrath of Innocence 6
Christmas Truce..7
Nothing but Brave..8
A Mother's Prayer..9
Grey Thoughts..10
Young Bloodlust..11
For the Love of the Land 13
Soldier Boy...15
The New Frock 17
Hunger at the Front 18
The "Warrior Mind" 19
Prophets 20
The Sword...21
Children Fair 22
The Generals...23
In Our Backyard 24
Cost 25
Battle Cries 26
A Soldier No More..27
My Friend 28
Trojan 29
The Lonely Soldier 30
Left for Dead 31
Victory Parade...32

Gas Masks..33

Hatred..34

War Poem 37

The Peace We Truly Seek.....................................38

Prophecy of the Fallen..39

The Mothers of War..40

The Lamb 41

Yesterdays, Todays, and Tomorrows.....................42

For the Tragedy of Reasoning...............................43

On Her Birthday...44

Meant to Be 45

In the Holy Father's Name 47

Loved Ones...48

His Love..49

Only God..50

The Soldier's Psalm 52

Ode to Death and Glory 53

Her Pride and Joy...54

Poppy Seeds 55

Battle Torn...56

Our Heroes Gone..57

Bravest Sons 58

The Monarch of the Realm 59

Soldier Mine 60

Call to Arms 61

Workhouse Pals...62

The Bell 63

On Murky Day 64

My Sweetheart Brave..65

The Sun Shines Once Again 66

C'est l'amour, C'est la Guerre 67

The Old Soldier 68

Boy on the Bus..69

A Soldier Unknown..70

The Enemy 71

The Witchypoo...72

Once Upon a Tragedy 73

The Broken and the Lost..74

The Dead of War 75

Songbirds 76

The Dardanelles...77

Man of War 78

The Final Whistle 79

The Somme..80

Grandfather Sweet...81

Soldier Gay 82

Soldier On...83

Final Note 84

By the Waves..85

That November Morn..86

The Sacred Poppy..87

The Gate..88

Mother Dear 89

The Fallen 90

Oh Why?! Oh Why?!...91

The Worst of Things..92

Final Act 93

Fallen as Thee 94

Out of the Trench 95

So Absolute 96

No More 97

Within the Field of Conflict 98

Coming Back 99

All Politics Aside 100

Our Glorious Dead 101

Each a Hero 102

The Finest Example 103

Little Lad 104

There's No Place like War 105

For What Know I? 106

Tomorrow at Dawn 107

The Sound of Fear 108

Of Sea and Flame 109

Commands 110

Remember Me 111

We Must 112

Christmas Came Early 113

No-Man's Land 114

The Lost Cause 116

The Sky 117

A Hero So Beloved 118

In the Clouds 119

Beyond Repair 120

He Did Well 121

With Love and Kind Regards 122

The Loss of a Feather 123

A Fallen Soldier 124

Victory 125

A Prayer for the Fallen 126

Onwards 127

Such Heroes 128

The Summer of Our Goodbyes 129

The Answer 130

They'll Always Stand Tall 131

Three Kings 132

Sword and Chalice 133

The Hunters 135

The Unslammable Door 136

Within the Mud 137

Within the Trench 138

The Taking of Passchendaele 139

The Ultimate Sacrifice 140

Present and Correct 141

The Dachshund 142

The 11th Hour 143

Praise Be 144
Out, Standing, in the Field 145
As the Sun Began to Rise 146
For the Very Last Time 147
By the Pretty Watermill 148
As They Fell 149
For What It's Worth 150
Lest We Forget 151
Ireland's Finest 152
Daffodils of the Valleys 153
The Thistle 154
The English Rose 155
Sweet Flowers 156
Sunset 157

Introduction

We must always disrespect war
But never the protagonists
For 'tis only they who know
What true agony is

—D. Stead, 23.7.2015

The Fortunes of War

Huddled in the freezing trench,
Their nostrils assailed
By a deathly stench.
Then blow the whistles,
And it's over the top,
Each one praying
For the horrors to stop.
Facing the same nightmare
Each morn they'd awake.
Thousands having drowned
In the soft mud lakes.
A few left now,
Sharing their last cigarettes,
Remembering the slain.
Too much to forget.
Ten million men,
Who bravely faced death.
Ten million men,
Too young drew last breath.
Ten million men,
All taken so young
By the bayonet, shell, or the gun.
Ten million men who went to fight,
Ten million heroes who are no more,
And how did we describe such awful plight?
"The fortunes of war."

16.1.2014

Home

Each was promised a home 'fit for a hero'.
They left behind their dim hovels
So each could fight so hard in the mud.
Then, praying for safety, would grovel
To stop further spilling of blood.

Returning with broken minds and hearts,
So tortured, lost, and alone.
Incapable of going back to home and hearth,
They were all simply placed in a "home".

2.12.2014

The Raven

We so quietly said our prayers,
With battle about to begin,
As said the enemy theirs,
All hoping to keep our fears within.
For the devil was misbehaving,
Since the horror didst begin.
For the war, it was the Raven,
And the Raven was called sin.

24.5.2016

Pie

Since 1914 they've served us pie,
Each time with a new flavour of sauce.
Every time we'll gladly give it a try,
Much to our bitter regret, of course.

Eagerly, we ravenously devour this most unsavoury dish,
Knowing full well such poison makes so many suffer and die.
Yet we keep eating as much as the politicians so wish.
Anybody for anymore pie?

17.8.2014

A Hero of Conscience

A hero of conscience soon enlisted.
Carrying such fear, his heart weighed heavy.
To hide his woes, false enthusiasm persisted,
Seemingly glad to do the same as so many.

Expected to go toward the enemy line
And fight an equally patriotic foe,
He couldn't face the consequences of staying behind,
Although he knew 'twas idiotic to go.

The Great War cut him down but not by his own will.
Knowing this shambolic war was such profound nonsense,
Unlike others so gloriously, heroically killed,
He simply died as a hero of conscience.

30.9.2014

The Wrath of Innocence

The wrath of innocence
Is never truly observed
By minds so insanely unbalanced,
Those without intention to serve.

Such sufferance of mind
Must be part of some greater plan
For those left behind
By each fallen man.

God knows 'tis so senseless
And serves no purposeful gain
For armies to fight so defenceless
Just to serve general pain.

Pity befalls women who bore
Those with minds amok with ferocity.
Who would bestow this horror-war,
Which is simply another word for atrocity?

Such wrongs shouldn't need righting
By those driven by arrogance,
Who keep reigniting
The wrath of innocence.

13.11.2014

Christmas Truce

For the sake of children, families, and mothers
Amidst worst of killing brought on by wrongful views,
To pause, from horrid war between brothers,
There came about a Christmas truce.

21.12.2014

Nothing but Brave

Serving with great honour and valour,
Every boy and very young man
Carried the weapons and banners
Of each one's nation-state flag.

All fought with such courage
As raging battles ensued,
And thus by war were so nourished
For 'twas only war that they knew.

The Great War
Ended November 11, 1918.
The vilest hell which they saw
Was even for Lucifer too obscene.

The brave had all lost,
For nothing was won.
For 'twas the brave who bore the cost
Of what wicked cowards had done.

The fallen were brave
And rest in an honourable grave.
But those who'd returned
Had to about peace once more learn.
For they'd known only war,
One way to behave,
So as like in wartime before,
They were nothing but brave.

4.7.2014

A Mother's Prayer

A mother's prayer, with parting sobs
While clutching linen handkerchief,
Was just one prayer to Almighty God
That the Great War would not bring her son to grief.

On a train departing full of steam,
Her only son waved, smiling from window open.
Her heart choked by most terrifying dream,
Yet still daring to dream that her son would not be taken.

The battlefield so sodden with blood was soaked.
Lord above, well why should He care?
On tears full of worry and love she choked,
Fearful her son would not come back to her.

Then, on darkest day, saddest telegram,
For God had been just so unfair.
In fact, He hadn't given a damn
Just to take a moment to listen to a mother's prayer.

29.9.2014

Grey Thoughts

In a few moments, I'll be gone,
As I'll die alongside brothers in arms,
Comforted that you are warm at home
And safe within your mother's arms.

As by machine-gun fire I'm cut down,
I know my soul shall rise towards heaven above.
As my body is dragged to hell by hellish hounds,
I'll ascend beyond death by way of your sweet love.

As whistles blow, I now go over the top.
I bid you farewell, my bonnie cairn.
Look after mother, my sweet little dog,
For very soon you'll be her only bairn.

Now, lying here as this shattered, bloody mess,
My life is all but ebbed away.
Last thoughts—goodbye, God bless,
My little dog, so grey.

9.10.2014

Young Bloodlust

In high summer 1916,
Sergeant had seen war without end.
Came a young boy soldier so green,
Sergeant promised, 'I'll protect my very young friend.'

Baptism of fire for the lad came soon.
After hostile exchanges were met,
Sergeant became head of platoon
For most were killed taking the enemy trench.

The lad was close to Corporal Lance.
Above battle noise, no one quite heard everything said,
So Sergeant gave a secondary glance,
And then the whole sordid story he read.

Corporal Lance had given the lad cigarettes
And placed his hand upon the youngster's shoulder.
'This, my lad, you won't regret.'
Then smiled at the "pretty" boy soldier.

Corporal Lance and the lad
Quickly disappeared out of sight.
Sergeant had to quickly react.
He needed all men once more to fight.

Lance and the boy met three others waiting.
'This isn't what you said before!'
Totally against what he'd been anticipating,
The three others pinned him to the floor.

He had not experienced such vile extremes
Amidst the Great War so abhorrently violent.
Close by, even more dying soldiers screamed,
But throughout his ordeal, he kept silent.

Through battlefield chaos, they'd somehow gone.
Lance and the others fled the Great War.
The youngster believed 'twas his doing wrong.
His spirit too broken to fight anymore.

He managed to stand, still completely stunned,
Struggling to smile, as Sergeant appeared,
Only to be facing a fixed-bayonet gun.
'You bloody coward, I know what you did here.'
'I just can't face it, Sarge!'
'Just get back to battle, you little queer!'
And with a rush towards the bayonet charged.
At which Sergeant choked backed tears,
And as Sergeant watched his friend die,
Thus realizing the events of that day.
He knew the truth had to be denied,
Knowing what he could never say
To his only son, 'Goodbye,'
As he laid him gently downwards to the dust
And tearfully whispered, 'Why,
Why must we have this, young blood lust?'

24.7.2014

For the Love of the Land

Soldier Private Donald Head,
Upon leaving for the Great War
To his small daughter said,
And wholeheartedly solemnly swore,

'Don't worry, sweet Anne
I promise that I'll be back.
Just look after your mam
And sweet little baby Jack.'

'Daddy please don't leave me,
Baby Jack, and our mam.'
'But sweet Anne, it has to be.
For God and the love of the land.'

Anne's daddy lies frozen cold
In an icy no man's land,
Stripped of his life and his soul
As so many a good soldier man.

Frosty Monday morn, in class,
Joyful Anne sat next to John.
Her joy was soon as shattered glass,
Her happy, sweet smile just gone.

Anne's mam had come through the door.
Tear-stained telegram in hand,
Coming from the Office of War,
Which was delivered directly to mam.

Mam's heart simply broke.
Too upset to read what it said,
So the trembling teacher spoke
The awful news, which she read.

'In midst of battle missing,
Regrettably presumed dead.'
For another man's name Anne was wishing,
But alas 'twas Private Donald Head.

Poor crying Anne screamed, 'Why?
Daddy promised me he'd be back.
How could God tell such a lie
And murder such a sweet, decent man?
How could God send Daddy to die?
Surely not for the love of the land!'

7.7.2014

Soldier Boy

'Why have they sent
This feeble young pup
Who seems hell-bent
On trying to grow up?'

'Why, he'd be drunk
On half a pint of weak beer.
He hasn't the spunk
To last half a week around here.'

At the tender age
Of just-turned twelve,
He marched toward the rage
Of the Great War-hell.

To the apron strings
He should have been tied.
But, instead, he did and saw such horrible things
On his very young way to die.

So many fell in battle
By day and by night.
Slaughtered like cattle,
Having no choice but to fight.

It was breaking his heart,
All the horror and the hurt,
When a bullet-shaped dart
Ripped straight through his shirt.

As he fell to the ground,
He cried out for his mum.
But with all-out carnage around,
He knew no one would come.

As he lay there shaking,
His young life destroyed,
One of ten million taken
Was fallen, brave, soldier boy.

17.6.2014

The New Frock

Mrs May Brown
Went into the shop.
She seemed so down,
Her heart a big rock.

'Why, Mrs Brown,
What a surprise!
Why are you so down,
With tears in your eyes?'

'My boy Albert
Went off to the Great War,
But I've just heard
He won't be home anymore.

'Please excuse the tears,
My pretty young miss,
It's just … he was shot, I fear,
For complete cowardice.'

'How about our latest line
Of lovely new frocks.
A very pretty design
Called … Total Shell Shock.'

30.6.2014

Hunger at the Front

'The warmongers
We're such a small group now
And we have such hunger
Yet they won't even send soup now

Perhaps with some sausage
That would fill a hole
It would be worth all of our losses
For even a very small bowl'

'Unless I'm mistaken
I smell eggs and bacon.'

'You're sadly mistaken
For want of bacon and eggs.
That smell isn't bacon
But rotting war dead.'

21.2.2015

The "Warrior Mind"

In high summer 1914
Came such a war,
The like of which was never seen,
By man nor beast before.

'Twas war to end
All others,
Thus killed were our friends,
As we slaughtered our brothers.

After four years bore
Sixteen million war dead,
But the war to end wars
Was a lie we'd been fed.

Heroes returned with true reality of war,
Heroes cast aside, as if rancid dog faeces,
Their cost higher than had profit bore,
For 'twas always the nature of our species.

War dead, war wounded, war blind,
We have through our existence mourned,
Since the very dawn of mankind,
For each and all are born,
Possessing the "warrior mind".

10.7.2014

Prophets

Prophets spoke so much political rhetoric.
After all these politicians were wise.
And hence brought forth the Great War so chaotic.
Still, no one really opened their eyes.

Each token leader had laid claim:
'You'll fight on the side of God and truth.'
And was true. Yet not had these orders from this world came
But from he with the cloven hoof.

To millions dying just totally blind,
All they ever regarded was an increasing margin.
To know one thing they were ever truly inclined
To be sure their aim kept enlarging.

So many years since the end of the Great War,
And yet humanity has learnt nothing from it
Apart from, to carry on as before
And simply be ruled by PROFITS!

1.10.2014

The Sword

The sword of power
'Twas always used to hack, not to heal
Throughout this blood-soaked history of ours
By whoever wouldst the sword wield.

So oft, as oft times before
Proud mothers' brave heroes have not come back.
So let's not use the sword to cause war.
Let's use it to heal, not to hack.

17.8.2014

Children Fair

Her children fair
Went off one day
With their mother's care
Lovingly waving them away

Toward fields awash
With filth and mud,
Her only want
To bestow her love.

She wished for them the very best.
Alas her dreams as sombre ashes fell,
Her hopes dashed as they all met death
Throughout four years of bloody hell.

Once these babes were gone
'Twas her cross to bear,
The cherubs she'd taught to be so strong
Her beautiful, children fair.

21.12.2014

The Generals

A general, so politically wrong
Drove this war upon its evil course.
Young men so drunk by patriotic song
Made charge aback apocalyptic horse.

A general, named general gain
Directed complete chaotic slaughter,
The only victor, general pain
And a bloodied prize, awash with tear-stained water.

Totalling far and above
A completely priceless cost,
Those who'd loved,
And loved ones lost.

A futile war
Of nothing great,
The greatest general
General waste!

9.1.2015

In Our Backyard

In our backyard
So many years ago
So many were coming to harm
Via bloodthirsty military show.

By sixteen million dead it was measured,
Soon after happening again.
Millions more killed just so treasured
Women, children, and men.

Wars that were said to mean something
In memory of those who'd suffered so.
In reality, what was good was nothing,
Don't let it bother you though.

We remember those cruelly taken,
But time goes by, so it doesn't hit us so hard.
If you believe war has stopped since you're sadly mistaken,
Because it's "NOT" in our backyard?!

29.10.2014

Cost

As day
Is a reflection of night,
Darkness
Is a reflection of light.
As hope
Is a reflection of loss,
Freedom
Is a reflection of cost.

29.7.2015

Battle Cries

The battle cries given
When going into battle
By the cause of war further driven
Shredded nerves to a rattle.

The weather so cold
Like their souls
Could be warmer.
Into hell they'd been sold
Toward tormented trauma.

Each night thereafter, for years
They would sleep,
Re-awakening such terrors
So real and so deep,
And every night
A new horrid surprise,
Reliving old wounds
And suppressed ones reprised.
Remembering in dreams each one
As they so painfully and so horribly die,
Screaming to God
Who never replies,
Waking in sheer panic
With tears in their eyes,
Uttering one word
And that word being 'why?'
These are the real
Battle cries.

26.2.2014

A Soldier No More

As I walked into Civvie Street
And went through the door
I saw my wife and small children so sweet
And became a soldier no more.

I see my comrades once again
As I remember what I saw
Their tortured faces crying in pain
Then I awaken a soldier no more.

All memories have now vanished
The ghastly horror of war.
I am as fallen comrades vanquished
And finally, a soldier no more.

4.9.2015

My Friend

As we came face to face
With hateful terror in our eyes,
We danced entwined, in deathly embrace,
Both trying to stay alive.

I cared not, if had he child or wife,
With no worry for their names,
Trying to take each other's life
Was our one and only aim.

As he fell toward the ground,
His war and life both met their end,
My erupting tears made silent sound,
For a man who could have been my friend.

16.9.2015

Trojan

War snappeth the mind
And puts the heart asunder.
For the warrior doth not ever find
Safe shelter from the thunder.

For whatever life he first knew
War hath his innocence broken
For he, battles will always ensue.
Forever more he fights on as a Trojan.

8.9.2015

The Lonely Soldier

When into battle he doth go,
The soldier leaves his mark behind,
For when ready to meet the foe,
An eerie solitude will find.

But despite the once comradely laughter,
For sake of war, can humanity never atone,
So, since war's end thereafter,
The soldier is always alone.

23.3.2016

Left for Dead

Each agonising cry
I cannot but forget,
Of whose swift end I didst deny,
My comrades who were left,
In no-man's land to lie,
For they remain within my head.
Just not brave enough was I,
To help those left for dead.

26.5.2016

Victory Parade

We waved, and cheered
So loud that day
As they marched away,
So proud and brave.

And as their heels rained
So hard upon the ground.
Small laughing children played
In our pretty little town.

Then soon, one by one,
Arrived the telegrams,
To say a husband or a son
Was a fallen man.

So in our tiny church we prayed
For the fallen in their graves,
And a sorrowful piper played
A sombre, sad lament
For our very few returning men,
Such was our victory parade.

4.10.2015

Gas Masks

Somebody shouted:
'Everybody back.
The enemy's launching
A gas attack.'

Worried and confused
Some of them asked:
'Have we any to use
Of these so called gas masks?'

Very soon
They'd all gone blind,
And unable to see
Any gas masks to find.

Shortly afterwards
No one could breathe,
For headquarters hadn't bothered
Any gas masks to leave.

And finally,
Nothing more to be said,
Because they had no gas masks,
They were all bloody dead.

16.7.2015

Hatred

Burning hatred filled our hearts
So bright as to lust the kill,
And so we tore the enemy apart,
For we had no other will.

Any man could not but more agree
And admit to be sick of the sight,
But yet we committed further horrors obscene,
When amidst the thick of the fight.

End of war such was our aim,
Comrade and enemy alike.
Very sadly all the living were maimed,
Quite badly by each man that died.

Feeling dazed, 'twas beyond belief,
Yet no victory had been won,
Although we felt such relief,
Our hatred simmered on.

8.9.2015

We must all strive,
To be soldiers of peace
So peace can truly thrive
And to put mankind's soul at ease.

But for peace to be maintained,
We must but search our souls to the core,
For whilst wickedness remains
We must always be ready for war.

13.1.2016

"Accidents
And wars,
They don't just happen.
They are caused."

13.1.2016

War Poem

As we are heading
To a point in time
Where we face Armageddon,
For we seem so inclined
With the fallen laying
In mud and slime
Over bodies decaying,
Even more warriors climb
On battlefields haunted
With bloodlust in mind.
They pick up the gauntlet
Whilst writing each line
That keeps mankind taunted
By persistent war rhyme.

9.2.2016

The Peace We Truly Seek

With violent images in our minds
From warriors to the meek,
Will we ever find
The peace we truly seek?

24.2.2016

Prophecy of the Fallen

The fallen have shown the way
By telling warlike what will ensue,
But alas somehow every day
Starts horrid war anew.

The fallen have explained
To those who would cause war,
Multitudes will be slain
If they continue as before.

Those who are at fault
Have within their capacity
To bring about a halt
Thus ending the fallen's prophecy.

14.1.2016

The Mothers of War

I shot men who could've been my brothers
As they lay dying ignored
The almighty Lord
And in last moments implored
Tender love from their mothers.

Bringing forth a sad shame
And always ending the same,
Yet again and again
As oft times before
'Tis usually men
That are the mothers of war.

15.5.2015

The Lamb

The Great War—it had come
Because of enemy so reviled.
He bade farewell to his only son,
His one and only child.

As he tended to the flock,
His soldier son tended bullet wound
Soon to pass away from shock,
Young life ended too soon.

Mother placed something in his hand,
As he prepared to tend his sheep,
He read the tragic telegram,
Then he shuddered and began to weep.

He found it hard his flock to tend
As the sun shone across the land.
His broken heart could never mend
For he'd sacrificed the lamb.

16.9.2015

Yesterdays, Todays, and Tomorrows

In their yesterdays, they believed
They could not falter.
Their todays were taken
Amongst the slaughter,
Thus their tomorrows sacrificed
Upon hell's altar.

22.9.2015

For the Tragedy of Reasoning

For the tragedy of reasoning
The papers came through the door.
They all understood the meaning then.
He must fight in the Great War.

As their hearts were slowly sinking,
From their eyes tears began to fall.
Of his children he tried to be thinking
But he had to answer the call.

He said he must now be leaving them
To protect all that they had known,
And for the tragedy of reasoning
He never again came home.

15.1.2016

On Her Birthday

On her birthday, party day,
The Great War didn't seem to matter.
She smiled and laughed, so jolly and gay,
But her world was about to shatter.

They'd made a cake for the child's party,
The giggling little Rosa,
But as she laughed aloud and hearty,
The bombs came ever closer.

Because of war, they ran for their lives,
Then called out their little girl's name.
They worried for her, being only five,
But they searched for her in vain.

Her grubby face, her hair a mess
While wandering lost in danger zone,
Wandering bewildered in dirty lilac dress,
And crying to go home.

Then sobbing, 'Mummy, it's my birthday!'
While entangled in barbed wire,
Sadly, she slipped away,
Caught up in the crossfire.

8.2.2016

Meant to Be

'Twas meant to be,
That my sons loved me so,
But for the nation's need,
My eldest son had to go.

I prayed for the love of God
For my youngest to stay with his mother
But my youngest's want
Was to follow his brother.

I learned of my youngest, lost to war,
By way of telegram sent to me,
Taken, as his brother, fallen before,
Dear God, why was it meant to be?

17.5.2016

For God, King, and Country

Für Gott, Kaiser, und Vaterland

In the Holy Father's Name

As warriors battle again once more
As in past times had they came,
Meeting again in acts of war,
In the Holy Father's name.

Like the Saviour Jesus Christ,
And Abel is once more killed by Cain,
Mother's children are sacrificed,
In the Holy Father's Name.

So battle plans can be aligned
War takes the Saviour's love in vain,
And God's commands are redefined,
In the Holy Father's Name.

To see the light of another day
And not to be cast towards hell's flame,
Down upon our knees we pray,
In the Holy Father's Name.

31.3.2016

Loved Ones

Such multitudes are gone,
And we know somehow
They committed nothing wrong.
For we know now
For want of war
Such ghastly plague.
What was it done for
If not deathly gain,
All merely sent to die
Amidst worst kind of hell?
God gathered their souls so far upon high
As our loved ones fell.

2.9.2015

His Love

His love, gave God
As their blood was spilled,
When going over the top
For all were wrongly killed.

'Twas never God's plan
For mankind to spill blood,
But war 'tis nature of man,
Yet God still giveth His love.

25.2.2016

Only God

Every brave soldier lad,
Had Cain's will to slay his brother,
And four other things did each have:
God, guts, luck, and each other.

But God had to abstain,
For He could not at all decide,
So only didst God's love remain,
For He could not take a side.

And the horror of Great War
Brought such horrific stalemate
For all humanity didst ignore,
That only God is great.

1.7.2016

If you solemnly believe in God,
You cannot in the slightest believe in war,
But if you in slightest believe in war so wrong,
Then you ought not believe in God anymore.

3.7.2016

The Soldier's Psalm

A few, unjustly, are so pious
And act holier than thou,
Having drawn up darkest of hell's fires,
So the Great War rains down upon us now.

And we know Almighty God doth love us
As we pray for our Saviour's help,
But even He cannot protect us from above us,
So how best do we save ourselves?

For amidst such vile insanity,
We are plunged into the way of harm,
So we shall fight for all humanity,
Now having read, our soldier's psalm.

1.7.2016

Ode to
Death and Glory

Death is the chariot
Upon which warriors sit
Drawn by glory
Which is such tragic myth.

22.9.2015

Her Pride and Joy

Her pride and joy,
A promise they had made,
Her young and handsome soldier boys
Had promised to stay safe.

There came a knock upon the door.
Had they their promise kept?
Thinking they were home once more
Her heart, it simply leapt!

But her sons did not stand there.
Instead, solitary soldier man.
Her heart sank with despair
As she took both telegrams.

For her sons that she'd adored
Had left her so bereaved
Because of the Great War
Their loss she sadly grieved.

They'd left her all alone,
Her heroic twin soldier boys,
They were not returning home,
Her sons—her pride and joy.

22.2.2016

Poppy Seeds

History says
Back in days before,
With their lives they paid
Because of war.

After hellish war
Peace anew
And from bloodied soil
A poppy grew.

Such bravery there never was
As had these fallen men,
And so give thanks unto dear God
'Twas not us but them.

With bravery unbeknown,
Which served our nation's needs,
We're so grateful they were sown,
Our fallen poppy seeds.

4.2.2016

Battle Torn

Battle torn are the soldiers
Whom we'll carry forever more
Upon our nation's shoulders
As in times gone by before.

We'll keep the home fires burning
For our heroes dead and not yet born,
And for heroes continually returning
From war, so battle torn.

5.6.2016

Our Heroes Gone

Our heroes gone remember with pride,
Those who'd fought so hard and long,
Remembering for us they bravely died,
So let's honour our heroes gone.

18.7.2016

Bravest Sons

Not one hero
Is now left,
Yet no one
Should them forget,
And the horror of Great War
Once done,
Which befell our nation's
Bravest sons.

30.7.2016

The Monarch of the Realm

We shall risk death
So vile and obscene
With very last breath
For our sacred queen.

As in times before
Our forbears did such things
In every act of war
For queens and kings.

For swiftly we shall run so fast
Into the flames of hell,
Holding out until the last
To protect, the Monarch of the Realm.

20.6.2016

In honour of
Her Majesty Queen Elizabeth II

Soldier Mine

Soldier mine who shine so bright,
Who was the bravest of the fight,
Now thou art fallen, as the night.

Although so near, thou art so far,
Far away as shining star.
Your battles, they be ended, for all time,
So shine forever, soldier mine.

4.10.2015

Call to Arms

Call to arms
Everyone kept hearing,
So away they marched
While the crowds were cheering.

They couldn't help longing
To be safe and warm,
As they found themselves running
Through the fire-storm.

Then thinking of loved ones
While in the way of harm,
They heard quite a different
Call to arms.

19.10.2015

Workhouse Pals

They'd no idea what lay in store
When signing up on the day,
So onwards towards war
They heartily marched away.

Through a rain of hell
They became so brave.
The generals cared not who fell,
Even though so many were under age.

The Great War paid them a great insult,
So let's remember them now,
The boys who'd through war became adults,
The heroic, workhouse pals.

20.11.2015

The Bell

And so fell
A freezing rain shower,
As fast approached
The darkest hour.

Behind dark clouds
Had the sun disappeared,
As we braved whistle sounds
'Twas not God we feared.

Once over the top
We ran at random,
By then, knowing by God
We'd been abandoned.

Amidst the horror
Of terrifying hell we revelled,
When we rang the bell,
Which awakened the devil.

10.12.2015

On Murky Day

On murky day, he stepped down,
From a steaming train.
Seemed so different his home town,
Although nothing had but changed.

It started to rain so light,
As two small boys with a football played,
He caught glimpses of such horrific sights,
At which became his mind so plagued.

As he knocked upon the door,
Of this moment had mother dreamed,
Laughing 'You're back home from war,'
But all he heard were screams.

Back home to family once more,
But alas, had he not survived,
Sadly, still battling the Great War,
Forever raging, in his mind.

24.2.2016

My Sweetheart Brave

My sweetheart brave
Has gone to war
As heroes marched away
Many times before.

I dread the day
That I may learn
My sweetheart brave
Shall not return.

24.12.15

The Sun Shines Once Again

When the sun shines once again,
For clouds of war are in the sky,
I'll see you safe at home with me then,
So it's farewell and not goodbye.

As I open each letter
I breathe sigh of relief,
But I feel only slightly better,
For it's your safe return I seek.

There came sorrowful telegram to the door
To tell of my fallen husband brave,
And since end of the Great War
I lay flowers upon your grave.

And as you sit next to God
As so many other brave soldier men,
I wish my days of sorrow gone
So that the sun shines once again.

26.2.2016

C'est l'amour, C'est la Guerre

In love and war
All is but fair.
Heroes rush in
Where fools wouldn't dare.

Because 'twix war and love,
Is far too much to bear,
For love and war are such,
C'est l'amour, c'est la guerre.

23.1.2016

The Old Soldier

Because there came the call
A brave man marched to war,
And for the sake of his young love stood tall,
So as to prove his love forever more.

Returning home with joyous glee,
He praised the Lord above,
Knowing his sweetheart again he'd see,
For he was so happy to be in love.

Her words seemed so unfair
That he had nothing to offer her,
And that his love could not compare,
To her young and handsome officer.

Her hurtful excuses he could not take
And asked her to speak no more,
For what she was saying was heavier heartache
Than horror he'd felt during the Great War.

Because of such cruel words spoken.
Gone was the reason for his life,
With the brave warrior's hearts so broken
The old soldier simply died.

11.7.2016

Boy on the Bus

Young boy on the bus
Yearned for military quest
So asked question of old man
With medals adorning his chest.

'Did you fight …
… in the war?'
'Yes, that's right,
And the one before.'

The boy said: 'I want
To fight in a war.'
The old man said:
'No you don't! What for?'

The boy replied:
'To go for glory
—or to die!'
'But it's no adventure story,
Perhaps soon you'll see why.'

The boy got off
And went on his way
And entered into a shop.
Not for long did he stay.

For a picture saw he within the shop
Of shot soldier falling backward to die,
Titled with eternal question.
'Why?'

23.5.2016

A Soldier Unknown

As upon the battlefield he lays.
A fallen soldier's courage is shown,
So to God in heaven give praise,
And endearment to a soldier unknown.

9.12.2015

The Enemy

My brother quickly I pushed safe
Because of bombs sent by the hun,
My lower leg was blown away.
To save my life, he had to run.

He'd gone for help, whereas I could not,
My brother, being more than a friend to me,
But was killed by fearful officer-shot,
Alas, mistaken for the enemy.

21.11.2015

The Witchypoo

The witchypoo so repellent
Reared her ugly head
And gave blood-curdling shriek triumphant,
Standing atop mountain of the dead.

Came final push upon the hag,
And after four years of wintry war,
She lay smashed and broken upon the crag
And a hopeful spring sprang forth.

25.3.2016

Once Upon a Tragedy

Once upon a tragedy
Because there came the call
Which was of course a fallacy
Causing ten million to fall.

The reason for such magnitude,
The fallen lost so tragically,
Was caused by those who had ineptitude
Once upon a tragedy.

15.1.2016

The Broken and the Lost

The broken and the lost
By war are created,
For token words should not
Cause more of the world to be devastated.

Too many wise words
Are left unread,
Written for us
By the foresight of war's dead.

Too many meaningful words
Are left unspoken about war's cost,
A cost which brings upon this world
The broken and the lost.

12.11.2015

The Dead of War

What more
Can be said
Of war's
Millions of dead?
Forever more,
Could one ask why,
But the dead of war
Speak so much louder than I.

27.5.2016

Songbirds

Sang so many less songbirds
By sombre November morn.
There were no befitting words
To honour the dead and gone.

A torch gone out of blazing hell
That left so many poor souls dead
Which had engulfed the entire world
Leaving sixteen million songbirds less.

17.2.2016

The Dardanelles

Inspired by romantic notions
And heroic ideas in his mind,
He left home, 'caused by patriotic devotions,
But sadly tragedy did find.

He so tearfully could not stop
Thinking of mother and little Jessica,
Then with next wave, went over the top,
As part of continual massacre.

He had no understanding
Whilst dying amidst such hell
Of why they'd made the landings,
At Gallipoli, on the Dardanelles.

4.2.2016

Man of War

Man of war he'd hoped to be
To serve a hopeful nation,
Not knowing outcome held for he
Alongside fallen generation.

So heroic man of war was slain,
Returning home not more,
Lost in battle to remain,
Forever, man of war.

3.5.2016

The Final Whistle

Together two sides doth clash,
Upon fields so soaked with blood,
For 'tis bigger than any other match,
Alas not the game I love.

For here, the arsenal creates destruction,
Yet we are united to protect each city,
For sake of warring instructions,
Which only creates more sorrow and pity.

'Tis sombre endgame held for me,
As over the top we soon shall go,
I so wish were still I referee,
As I, the final whistle blow.

21.5.2016

The Somme

Walking, toward the enemy, their time, they would take,
Wrongly thinking, empty each German trench,
But aghast when knowing such huge mistake,
'Twas far too late to turn their heads.

Both shells and men would scream and wail,
While army chaplains read out psalms.
The battle raged on biblical scale,
As thousands fell into the Saviour's arms.

Of most infamous battle, of Great War
Their names be left in poem and song,
And inscribed in heaven forever more,
Those who fell upon the Somme.

29.4.2016

Grandfather Sweet

Grandfather sweet had hardly enough,
Yet gave his abandoned baby grandson a home.
In a house holding not much, except love,
The old man raised the boy as his own.

Called by the Great War, his teenage boy was thrilled,
As grandfather sweet shook his head,
Shortly afterward, discovering his grandson was killed,
By way of sad telegram he'd been sent.

Grandfather sweet sat down upon the doorstep,
Knowing his boy he'd never more see,
And the kindly old man uncontrollably wept,
For so heartbroken was grandfather sweet.

17.7.2016

Soldier Gay

He didn't seem the type
Who would a woman fancy,
So we beat him up one night
As we all shouted "Nancy".

But with the enemy shells
The tension became so heightened,
And through a living hell
We all became so frightened.

Because we could not
He led the assault
And to the ground dropped
Because of bullet he'd caught.

Who'd have thought
He'd save our lives that day
And we're all still here, to talk
Of our comrade fallen—soldier gay.

2.8.2016

Soldier On

Soldier on, a front line telephone,
Said: 'Sir! Headquarters, for you.'
Hearing orders that chilled him to the bone,
The tragic outcome he then knew.

Thinking there was a way through,
Headquarters thinking, was so muddied.
'Twas their ridiculously insane view,
To "push on" with murder so cold-bloodied.

The officer turned to his men and said:
'I'll now lead you over the top.
Please try not to be upset,
For we must bravely soldier on.

4.8.2016

Final Note

As I use father's pen and fine ink,
And only page of Mother's Bible she'd sent,
My tears doth rapidly drip
Upon passage reading: 'Jesus wept.'

God sends His tears from the sky
For those who have fallen already,
But I must wholeheartedly try
To hold myself so steady.

Readying my nerves for no-man's land,
Dreading my climb from out of the trench,
Knowing I'll soon shake death by the hand,
My knotted stomach becomes ever more wrenched.

For we are about to attack
On this freezing morn of November,
And now there is no turning back
In my final moments, so sombre.

Now, that I have been caught by time,
I hurriedly scrawl with lump in my throat,
For 'tis my saddest goodbye,
By way of this final note ...
... "whistles".

3.7.2016

By the Waves

By the waves of their loved ones
They were waved away to war,
So many, so young and handsome,
Were to be seen never more.

Twas a sailors worst dream,
Jutland's battle hell,
And each man's dying scream
Was akin to tragic tolling bells.

War had these men forsaken,
But their souls by God were saved,
The heroes who were taken,
At Jutland-by the waves.

8.9.2016

That November Morn

Yes, remember at eleven,
That November morn,
The feasting crows,
Poured further scorn,
Upon the dead,
Who'd just been born.
Yes, remember at eleven,
That November morn.

19.10.2015

The Sacred Poppy

For the sake of our beloved nation,
And to give lost heroes respect,
Our fallen must have salutations,
So we shall our sacred poppy protect.

31.7.2016

The Gate

In Belgium in the town of Ypres,
There is an inscripted arch,
Where descendants of the fallen weep.

The arch is called the Menin Gate.
And at sunset each eve
'The Last Post' is played,
As many for lost forefathers grieve.
Paying these heroes tribute
By the laying of red poppy wreathes.

When the buglars sound 'The Last Post',
One feels they're sounding a sorrowful knell,
To resurrect the ghosts
Of each tragic victim who fell.

So visit the Menin Gate Arch,
And you might just get a tiny taste,
Of what it was like for men who marched,
Towards death, through "HELL'S GATE"!

6.8.2014

Mother Dear

Thinking about our home, I dwell,
Yet my last dwelling place is here,
In this land of screaming shell,
My heart rapidly beats with fear.
Within this war-torn earthly hell,
As my impending death is near,
I now bid you a final, sad farewell,
My sweetest, mother dear.

26.8.2016

The Fallen

Forced to commit such ghastly acts,
Yet so bravely had they behaved,
Not knowing, with hell had they made a pact,
So now are by the light of heaven bathed.

So war could not the valiant mock,
Upon tears their mothers would weep,
God hath gathered souls of heroes lost,
So shall the fallen peacefully sleep.

2.4.2016

Oh Why?! Oh Why?!

Our weakest voice
Is that of battle cry.
Why do we make such choice?
Oh why?! Oh why?!

16.1.17

The Worst of Things

Creature of this world
Death thou doth breed.
Oh spawn of hell
Upon death thou feed.

You bare your teeth
Each morn, each night,
With monstrous reach
To all those in sight.

The world's hate thou doth bore,
For such vile rage you bring.
Oh war! Oh war!
Thou art the worst of things.

7.8.2016

Final Act

The time must surely come
When no more innocence is taken,
By calling of the drums,
By which the world is so violently shaken.

For one day shall finally rest,
The fallen in their graves,
Those upon whom the sun shall never set,
These shining hero warriors brave.

When, mankind will finally know
War's not needed anymore,
And then shall be played triumphant notes,
After the final act of war.

31.7.2016

Fallen as Thee

Now that the sun
Rests in the sky
And war is once again done,
Peaceful as the night.
Such are these things I know,
Which cannot comfort me,
But I'll not let war overshadow
Those fallen as thee.

20.8.2016

Out of the Trench

Some, like babes
For their mothers cried.
Others, they prayed
To dear God on high.

As the whistles blew
With such a screaming trill,
It was then we knew
To run across the killing field.

Each man so brave
Heroically fell the same,
Thus none were saved
When out of the trench we came.

18.9.2016

So Absolute

So absolute was the will
Of generals, themselves not willing
To send more young men to kill,
Amongst such absolute killing.

Already so many had died
With only one tactical condition:
Of each opposing side
To fight with complete attrition.

For this was their only ability,
For a victory so resolute,
In midst of complete futility,
Of a war, so absolute.

24.9.2016

No More

So many millions ran the gauntlet
Of the calling of Great War,
And so by war were thus anointed
That ten million ran no more.

26.9.2016

Within the Field of Conflict

Within the field of conflict,
Plays each hero in theatre of war,
But just as heroes fallen,
Returning heroes fight no more.

So bravely and so hard they fought,
Those who fell or not the same,
But heroes who fell or not
Within the field of conflict remain.

3.10.2016

Coming Back

Coming back had I such plans and dreams
Of a future so wondrous and bright,
But couldn't help seeing such horrid things,
When I closed my eyes at night.

Ever since, within my heart and mind,
I could not find the peace I lack,
In remembering war's horrors that I'd left behind,
Dear God, please stop them coming back.

3.1.2017

All Politics Aside

For sake of victory's name,
Each one had raised their glasses,
Yet in battle fell the same,
Each of the different classes.

Loved ones so solemnly wept
For the fallen who had died,
For the Great War it had swept
All politics aside.

1.1.2017

Our Glorious Dead

Our glorious dead
Who did us proud,
Women children and men,
Who doth speak so loud.

Speaking against act of war,
Hope hears what they have said,
Horrid indignation suffer they not more,
Live on, our glorious dead.

14.1.2017

Each a Hero

So many soldiers
Standing in a row,
Nations' hopes upon shoulders
O'er the top they'd go.

So many fallen,
Lying in a row
For answering the calling,
Each a hero.

14.1.2017

The Finest Example

At the setting
Of the sun,
We shan't be forgetting
Sacrifices done.

Running into hell they'd go,
Having the bravest spirits
The fallen have finest example shown,
For their bravery knew no limits.

10.1.2017

Little Lad

Little lad with biggest smile
Stood at the school gate,
Would always for the longest while
For his big brother wait.

One day such strong words were said,
And he wished not see me more,
And so I said, I wished him dead,
As I turned to march to war.

After going through the mire,
I was returning back,
Within me just the one desire,
Make amends with the little chap.

Mother met me at the garden gate,
And my heart it did but snap,
For God had taken my best mate.
Be at peace, my little lad.

10.1.2017

There's No Place like War

There's no place like home, one says,.
It should be a place, of safety known,
And bravest hearts, are kept so gay,
By thought of going home.

A nation's heroic fallen may lie
Away from home forevermore,
But only a warrior's heart shalt truly cry,
For there's no place like war.

16.1.2017

For What Know I?

As the sun
Has almost set
Which brings such vales of darkened glows,
The fallen we shall not forget.
I can only but suppose
Fates which heroic warriors met,
For what know I of those?

9.1.2017

Tomorrow at Dawn

Snatching sleep when we can,
We'd run for home if we could,
But every one of us a trench man
Must do what a good soldier should.

Our duty we must solemnly follow.
By our orders we shall abide,
For we shall run toward death's dark hollow,
Just as fallen comrades who'd died.

When whistles shall be blowing,
We'll wish for the day we were born,
For tonight we know we'll be going
To hell—tomorrow at dawn.

10.10.2016

The Sound of Fear

One might have been killed by fear,
For with a knife you could cut the air,
The only sound a few sorrowful tears,
And of course a few last-minute prayers.

Because over we would shortly be going,
As the last few seconds ticked by,
An almost certain fate each of us knowing,
Almost certain that each man would die.

'Twas a feeling so hard to explain,
For the near silence was so woefully loud,
Of such tortured hearts breaking with pain,
Yes, fear is such a terrible sound.

11.10.2016

Of Sea and Flame

Of sea and flame
So much they gave,
With so many lost
To watery grave.

Into water they were sent
As many mighty ships did drown,
Remembering the sailor dead,
Their comrades fathoms down.

So let's fathom out, 'tis disgrace
Of war that is to blame,
And of how in history, each took their place,
The heroes of sea and flame.

3.10.2016

Commands

Commands they were put forward,
By Deutschland, Le France, and Blighty,
As brave men proved themselves not cowards,
The politicians sat in palaces of the mighty.

The trench men saw not just the foe
Who would do to them such harm;
They saw an equal foe back home,
Which caused them much alarm.

But the generals simply ignored
The beleaguered men's demands,
And so an anguished lion with pain didst roar,
As a jackass gave commands.

25.11.2016

Remember Me

Remember me, for who I am,
Should I not return,
If by way of telegram
My death, you come to learn.

Please then, think of the son you had,
And when sister and I were small,
When we'd eat together bread and jam,
Before I grew to answer the call.

Treasure me as boy you raised,
For I have always treasured thee,
And if I should fall upon this day,
I beg, remember me.

25.11.2016

We Must

As fell down the winter snow,
So lit were final cigarettes
The sergeant said: 'Lads, it's nearly time to go,'
Then ordered: 'FIX BAYONETS.'

As the whistles blew that day,
Carrying with them, fear, greater than fear of God,
Within the trench young soldier stayed,
Tearfully screaming: 'Please make them stop!'

Clutching his crucifix to his chest,
'Boy, I know in God you trust.'
He sobbed: 'I don't want to leave the trench.'
'Come on boy, we must.'

12.10.2016

Christmas Came Early

No one could believe
The orders when they came,
The day before Christmas Eve,
That they'd go over the next day.

'I've made meatloaf and Christmas pud,'
Said their officer with tearful compassion.
"I'm sorry if it's not very good,
But it's the best I could do with my rations"

Christmas Eve then arrived
And within the men built up such fear,
Tragically, that morn each of them died.
That's why Christmas came early that year.

23.12.2016

No-Man's Land

With blowing of whistles, away we went,
Up the ladders, for 'twas our time,
My mind into a daze was sent,
As we left the trench behind.

Seeing horrors I'd never known,
My soul felt the deepest pain,
As around me the winds of hell didst blow,
My comrades fell tragically like rain.

As I ran across so many dead,
Such tears fell from my eyes,
And for taking those last fateful steps,
Forevermore in no-man's land I'll lie.

27.11.2016

War is
The greatest tragedy
Of human reasoning.

22.12.2016

The Lost Cause

As worst of battles ensued,
Amidst the most futile of wars,
The hopeful prayed to St. Jude,
The Patron Saint of the lost cause.

22.12.2016

The Sky

The sky was where
Upon airborne steeds,
Heroes fought an enemy there,
To serve a nation's need.

In the sky so blue and clear
They risked their lives above.
Far below, their sweethearts dear,
Young maidens so in love.

And in our hearts, they've won a place,
For in battle, heroes they didst die,
And so shalt never fall from grace
Those fallen from the sky.

27.10.2016

A Hero So Beloved

A hero so beloved
Is one who wouldst bring to us salvation,
But now rests in heaven above,
For heroically serving the nation.

Putting their lives in harm's way
Their loved ones could only worry,
Hoping they'd come home one day,
Yet to fight the enemy they'd hurry.

For each exalting prayer that's read,
For those in whom we've placed our trust,
Each of our fallen dead,
Is a hero so beloved.

1.12.2016

In the Clouds

In the clouds of smoke
I saw bravest of fighting men,
They were such a fine lot of blokes,
Whom I think of now and then.

From a war so deathly black
So few of my pals and I came home.
I was glad to have made it back,
But wish no one had had to go.

I think of where fallen comrades lay,
Those who fought and died so proud,
And I remember those darkest days,
When I see their faces in the clouds.

13.12.2016

Beyond Repair

'I'm sorry, son—it's beyond repair,'
Said young boy's sympathetic dad,
As toy soldier lay broken upon the stairs,
Which belonged to a crying small, wee lad.

The small, wee lad grew to march away
Alongside other brave soldier men,
As mother's tears fell like rain,
Begging God, 'Please bring him home again.'

Just as small wee lad with broken toy,
Mum and dad felt such despair,
For so smashed and broken came home their wee boy
That their hearts were beyond repair.

16.12.2016

He Did Well

By way of telegram didst she learn,
Of fallen son, lost at the front,
Never again wouldst he return,
As mother's heart and soul bore the brunt.

Knowing her boy was everything good and wholesome,
With pride her heart didst swell,
And knowing he fell, so young and handsome,
Like he, her eyes did well.

20.6.2017

With Love and Kind Regards

With telegram already two days received,
As snow lay upon the ground,
Came the post on Christmas Eve,
And her grief it didst compound.

Written out so tidy and neat,
She recognised the writing,
'Twas that of fallen son so sweet,
And her very soul felt struck by lightning.

'For a Merry Christmas, my sweet mum,
I've sent this handmade Christmas card,
As always, from your loving son,
With love and kind regards.'

30.5.2017

The Loss of a Feather

The loss of a feather so light,
Seems a small price to pay,
When lost in the fight,
For saving the day.

A white feather is given
To a coward it seems,
Yet to war must be driven
If himself is to redeem.

Let war end forever
As God doth hold sway,
For the loss of a feather
Is a price too high to pay.

27.5.2017

A Fallen Soldier

A fallen soldier
Has but war's blessing,
As war becomes even bolder,
And humanity learns no lessons.

When peace we finally see
And learn to accept her,
Then the spirit of peace
Can be no longer a spectre.

When angels weep
No more upon God's shoulder,
We'll know war's death cannot be,
Such as a fallen soldier.

26.5.2017

Victory

The victor 'twas always Mars,
The bringer of war,
With sorrow tragically ours,
So it would seem, forever more.

Then, as never before, had she seen us
Truly begin to love one another,
And as the world hailed a triumphant Venus,
In her arms she carried home her dead brother.

28.5.2017

A Prayer for the Fallen

For the fallen say a prayer,
For with Almighty God they rest.
They fell with bravery beyond compare,
So let us not them forget.

Just as our Saviour, Jesus Christ,
Let's show compassionate care,
Then purely a single candle light,
And for the fallen say a prayer.

26.5.2017

Onwards

Onwards, once out of the trench
With a prayer upon their lips,
Along with tears they had wept,
Across no-man's land,
Toward death they were swept,
Thus bravely fell going onwards
And have since in heaven slept,
They shalt forever march onwards,
For within our hearts they are kept.

13.6.2017

Such Heroes

To all those who'd in the Great War died,
From Jutland to Flanders Fields,
I know that I am so obliged
Before such heroes to kneel.

31.5.2017

The Summer of Our Goodbyes

The summer of our goodbyes
Was when Great War didst but start,
And such tears fell from her eyes
Because we had to part.

Hoping I'd return home at last
And hold her once again,
But all at once I felt such a blast
And didst lie amongst dead and dying men.

Although I'm alive, not much remains
Of the man whom I once was,
I'm thankful not to have gone insane.
Praise be to the grace of God.

My body, now but a useless sack,
By horror of war 'twas ravaged.
Send a telegram to tell: I shall not be back,
For I am but a wretch so ragged.

My arms and legs are sadly gone,
And have I no eyes with which to cry.
I wish the war had never come,
To bring the summer of our goodbyes.

15.12.2016

The Answer

A child asked of her mother,
'Why have wars to kill?
Why do this to each other?
Surely 'tis not God's will!'

'Why does God let so many die?'
She simply had to ask her.
Her mother tried not tell a lie:
'We're not meant to know the answer!'

19.12.2016

They'll Always Stand Tall

They'll always stand tall
Each of them so courageous
When answering the call,
Toward hell of war as to save us.

For angels will cry
Where heroes shall fall,
For where the fallen doth lie,
They'll always stand tall.

20.12.2016

Three Kings

Three Kings didst peace desire,
But for the sake of diplomacy inept,
'Twix those who wouldst conspire
With too many secrets kept.

So Great War it didst transpire,
For those who were so cherished,
Who fought so hard within the mire,
That ten million poor souls perished.

For the sake of so few liars
Many nations pay lasting respects.
For a war no one desired,
God has these fallen safe since kept.

15.2.2017

Sword and Chalice

The union of sword and chalice
Ought not peace hinder but help,
For when war brings its vile malice
Innocence suffers such torturous hell.

How is it God's heart is not broken
Whenever conflict doth but reign?
For peaceful words are seen to be token
When the world is engulfed by war's flame.

The two are united no more
Soon after the end of the fight,
But when again comes the onset of war,
Sword and chalice shall always unite.

17.2.2017

War serves one purpose,
If nothing else,
And of course, that one purpose
Is that war serves itself.

17.2.2017

The Hunters

The hunters became the hunted
When each to the front didst go,
By the Great War so repugnant,
Which consumed both comrade and foe.

For by such horrors were each confronted,
Sweet innocence lost in the hunt,
That the hunters became the hunted,
As they fell on the Western Front.

5.2.2017

The Unslammable Door

Two boys were raised in happy home
Whole family fearing God
Arguments were there ever none
A cross word there never was.

The eldest boy marched off to war
As father swelled with pride.
Mother prayed he'd be home once more,
As fearful tears she cried.

Younger boy at fourteen years old
Too young for war shan't follow,
He'd always done as he was told,
But now parental request seemed so hollow.

Then one night, so dark and grey,
He left a goodbye note,
And to Great War did run away,
After the door he did unbolt.

On eldest brother's return
There came hugs and reminiscing,
Although his parents eyes were burned
For his left leg was missing.

But a son had fallen amidst Great War
So came a tragic telegram,
But mother didst simply shut the door.
The unslammable door was slammed.

12.2.2017

Within the Mud

Fought so many within the mud,
Amongst the dying and the dead,
While in piles of paperwork, so stuck
A few generals shook their heads.

As each bomb fell with almighty thud,
They prayed so hard to Almighty God,
The dead and dying, within the mud,
Forget them we shall not.

6.2.2017

Within the Trench

Distant whistles one could hear
From enemy trench, not his own,
As trying with prayer to hold back tears,
He lovingly thought of home.

Trying in vain to protect themselves,
After some of the foe had gotten through,
It became each man for himself
As each tried all that he could do.

He was staring into the eyes of war,
And dread and fear came to his eyes,
So he stopped still to fight not more,
As he with fear became paralyzed.

As slain comrades and foe lay all about
So acquired he a heroe's understanding,
This lone soul who'd had no doubt
That he was the last man standing.

Mattered not whether comrade or foe;
The bravery of so many young heroic men
Was something only he would know
With the loss within the trench.

1.2.2017

The Taking of Passchendaele

The British had not succeeded,
As neither had the French,
So yet a further attempt was needed,
So Canadians poured from their trench.

Strange, ugly figures were the trees,
So black and horribly burnt,
Innocence dragged onto its knees,
Yet 'twas knowledge of enemy learnt.

The battles they were but so fierce,
Both sides trying so hard to win the day,
Their souls by terrifying horror pierced,
Yet wouldst fight on, come what may.

So remember always those who fell,
For they'd never us have forsaken,
On battlefields of bloody hell,
That led to Passchendaele being taken.

6.2.2017

The Ultimate Sacrifice

When a nation doth expect
Each to do or die,
In battle each must accept,
To face the ultimate sacrifice.

24.1.2017

Present and Correct

Ready for battle, all present and correct,
Many fine soldiers all in a line,
Standing to attention ready to inspect
In smart uniforms so fine.

Having fought the fiercest enemies,
Their bravery deserves such respect,
For now they lay in war grave cemeteries,
All present and correct.

2.2.2017

The Dachshund

In the land of Germany,
The dachshund felt alone,
And so he tried so heartily
To steal the treasured bone.

His situation became quite serious
And to keep he didst so yean
His power once imperious
But didst hard lesson learn.

For his luck was ending
After years of broken hearts.
A message they were sending
His people so torn apart.

As like leaving broken marriage,
He laid his fallen to rest,
And within a French train carriage,
The dachshund bowed his head.

9.2.2017

The 11th Hour

Let it be known
There's a whisper going round
That soon we'll go home
To our villages and towns.

From a war so wrong
That has torn each soul apart,
Yet still we must fight on
With such hurt within our hearts.

Upon battlefields so drenched
With blood and sacrifice,
We'll leave behind our fallen friends,
When the 11th hour strikes.

19.1.2017

Praise Be

A jolly and so playful boy
Wouldst for his mother sing,
Filling her heart with such joy
As church bells they didst ring.

Faithful to God were they,
As the boy to young man grew,
And bravely to Great War marched away,
Faithful toward the nation to.

The mother to the church she fled,
After painful news came to the door,
A telegram saying her son was dead,
Bravely fallen in Great War.

In front of Saviour, Jesus Christ,
She began to sob and cry,
For her child had been sacrificed,
But her heart understood not why.

And so, upon her knees,
She tearfully asked, 'Dear God,
How has this come to be?
Gone the joy of once what was
After faith I gave to thee.
Forgive me Lord, I must be gone,
For my fallen boy to grieve,
Knowing I'll never again hear his songs,
Yet for the son I had, praise be.'

28.2.2017

Out, Standing, in the Field

Out, standing, in the field,
Was a woman once so brave,
Whose heroism was revealed
By many lives she'd helped to save.

In this field of countryside farm,
Her efforts she recalled,
Remembering how she'd lost an arm
And those who didst but fall.

For Great War had brought such awesome fear,
And as a nurse she gave succour and shield,
And now and then she'd shed a tear,
For being outstanding in the field.

25.2.2017

As the Sun Began to Rise

Too fearful to fight anymore,
Young soldier suffering shellshock,
During hell of Great War,
At dawn, due to be shot.

Taken out and bound to a post,
As a prayer by army chaplain was read,
'Father, Son, and Holy Ghost,'
Then blindfold, knotted at back of head.

A volley of piercing shots rang out
Ending the young soldier's life,
In that instant a sole blackbird sang out,
As the sun began to rise.

8.4.2017

For the Very Last Time

For the very last time
I saw his smiling face,
Soldier son of mine,
When closing the garden gate.

I thought to myself,
'He'll be back' with a laugh,
As he ventured away
Along country path.

Of my fallen son
Each night I'd dream,
Of him returning home
As it should have been.

Now I have reached such an age,
For have passed so many years,
Yet each was just an empty page,
Since he fell, as have my tears

Forever more I'll be by his side,
Heroic soldier son of mine,
As I now come to close my eyes
For the very last time.

20.4.2017

By the Pretty Watermill

By the pretty watermill one day,
Young man and young girl met,
He swept the young girl's heart away,
And they knew their love would never end.

As mother poured tea into china cup
He'd heard of Great War's raging hell,
So he said, 'I'm joining up.'
And then came the wedding bells.

The young girl received a telegram
Saying her brave young husband was killed.
Then sobbed her heart out for her young man
By the pretty watermill.

21.4.2017

As They Fell

Becoming heroes so distinguished
Throughout hell of the Great War,
That each life which was extinguished
Is in God's keep forever more.

For eternity by His Hallowed Name,
Because of bayonet gun or shell,
Each of them became
Angels as they fell.

26.4.2017

For What It's Worth

For what it's worth, shed a tear,
For those who'd in Great War fought,
And maybe raise a glass of sombre cheer
And perhaps spare a little thought.

For the so many fallen dead,
And the poppy which sprang from the grave
In its resplendent bright blood red
After four years of acts so brave.

Please remember the fallen now and then
Who died amidst worst hell on earth.
Just shed one tear for all of them,
For what it's worth.

11.5.2017

Lest We Forget

Lest we forget the fallen,
The many brave heroes killed,
For war 'tis always calling,
For 'tis the devil's will.

Dying to keep the nation safe,
We forever owe greatest debt,
They fell fighting enemies at the gate,
Lest we forget.

1.12.2016

Ireland's Finest

Despite there being such apprehension
Amidst Great War, 'twas for sake of God,
And so with noblest of intentions,
Ireland's finest sons were lost.

2.1.2017

Daffodils of the Valleys

From the valleys they went,
And to foreign land did march.
Then, over the top, and out of the trench,
To fall, as brothers in arms.

Since, lying where the poppies grow,
Forever more they'll lie, so still,
Never more returning home,
Each one, a fallen daffodil.

23.1.2016

The Thistle

Finest tartan into hell was sent
At the blowing of the whistles,
And the edge of sharpest bayonet
'Twas so blunt against the thistle.

2.1.2017

The English Rose

The Great War didst test her mettle,
And brave Englishmen did fall,
But in losing her finest petals,
The English Rose stood tall.

2.1.2017

Sweet Flowers

Sweet flowers, by sweet women were thrown,
Saying farewell to soldier boys and men,
So many heroes had left behind home,
Never to see home again.

Of all those who'd answered the calling,
Ten million heroes was death's final yield,
So many brave boys who had fallen,
Now sleep beneath the poppy fields.

The Great War so vile and horrid,
Which lasted thousands of unbearable hours,
Had cut down such sweet flowers of the forest,
So let's remember ten million sweet flowers

5.8.2014

Sunset

Crimson red
In a blood-soaked sky,
Like wounded soldier
Lain down to die.

The sunset
Heralds end of day.
The wounded soldier
Passes away.

1.2008

In memory of the fallen, 1914 to present day.

Lightning Source UK Ltd.
Milton Keynes UK
UKHW012037110123
415201UK00012B/236/J